ON GOOD GROUND

ON GOOD GROUND

Poems & Photographs of Eastern Long Island

Edited by Ray Freed & Jim Tyack
Photographs by Ron Ribeiro

"As I view the leaf..." by David Ignatow was first published in *The Ontario Review* and is reprinted here with their permission.

"I saw a leaf flying..." by David Ignatow was first published in *The Paris Review* and is reprinted here with their permission.

"Sleepless" by David Ignatow first appeared in *Survivor's Manual* and is reprinted here by permission of its editor.

"First Day of Spring" by Robert Long is Copyright 1980 by *The New Yorker Magazine, Inc.*, and is reprinted here with their permission.

"Saying One Thing" by Robert Long, first appeared in *POETRY*, Copyright 1980 The Modern Poetry Association and is reprinted here by permission of the editor of *POETRY*.

"Private Eye" by Ron Overton first appeared in *The Ohio Review*, to whose editors grateful acknowledgement is made.

"The Front Gate" by Simon Perchik first appeared in *The Smith*, to whose editors grateful acknowledgement is made.

"The Beaded Pear" by Louis Simpson first appeared in the book *Caviare At The Funeral*, published by Franklin Watts, Inc. It is reprinted here with their permission.

L.C.C.C. No.: 81-50936

ISBN 0-935252-28-2

THE PRINT SHOP
Union Shop I.U. 450
333 Terry Road, Smithtown, N.Y.

STREET PRESS
Box 555
Port Jefferson, NY
11777

CONTENTS

MICHAEL BRAUDE / 6

The First Afternoon in a Village Called East Hampton / 7

VINCE CLEMENTE / 10

Clamming at Dusk / 11

JONATHAN COHEN / 14

Paumanok / 15

MICHELE CUSUMANO / 18

Love Affair and Altman's / 19

Blood Sandwiches / 20

GRAHAM EVERETT / 22

Thirteen, Full of Life / 23

The Potbelly Stove / 24

Grooming for Dinner with Death / 25

RAY FREED / 26

Moom: 3 / 27

Shinnecock Bay: 14 / 28

DAVID IGNATOW / 30

"As I view the leaf. . ." / 31

"I saw a leaf flying upwards. . ." / 32

Autumn Leaves / 33

Sleepless / 34

AARON KRAMER / 36

At Night / 37

NORBERT KRAPF / 38

Arriving on Paumanok / 39

ROBERT LONG / 40

First Day of Spring / 41

Saying One Thing / 42

DAN MURRAY / 44
August / 45
October / 46
A Toast to the Judge / 47

RON OVERTON / 48
Private Eye / 49

SIMON PERCHIK / 52
Today I Will Prepare the Ground / 53
The Front Gate / 54

ALLEN PLANZ / 56
Metro / 57

CAROL SHERMAN / 60
Sag Harbor / 61

LOUIS SIMPSON / 62
The Beaded Pear / 63

RUTH SWENSEN / 66
Living Inside My Body / 67

JIM TYACK / 68
The Invisible Rose / 69
Shadow / 70

JEANNE VOEGE / 72
The Whales in New York Harbor / 73

R.B. WEBER / 74
Summer Day along the Peconic
Behind These Lids / 76

CLAIRE NICOLAS WHITE / 78
Driving North on Nicoll's Road / 79
Lives / 80

ON GOOD GROUND

Michael Braude

THE FIRST AFTERNOON IN A VILLAGE CALLED EAST HAMPTON

Newcomer that you are in these parts,
you probably over-tipped the Schaeffer man . . .
but it pays off – he carries your bags into the 1770 House
not leaving before making sure you'll be accommodated.
The room they put you in could have been a mite bigger
but it does have its own bathroom, a walk-in closet,
a picture on the wall of Patrick Henry addressing the Burgesses
and, through the mullioned window, a view up and down Main Street.
The decor colonial – so authentic, so genuine –
you can almost hear Mister Henry asking for liberty or death:
the spell, if that's what it is, does not last,
restlessness sets in and you leave the room, walk downstairs,
stop off at the bar for a double scotch and go out the front door.
The air is fresh, a sharp tang to it,
the salt of ocean spray seasoning every breath you take:
a perfect day for a stroll – but where?
Newcomer that you are, instead of left, you turn right
and soon find yourself wandering among tombstones.
Death a theme tolerating but few variations,
deciphering epitaphs is still not unpleasant a pastime,
if somewhat repetitious . . . .
Hezekiah Brown is told to rest in peace,
so is Sherwood Fairweather, his wife Hepzibah;
so is Caleb Bufford and his two sons, Aaron and Mortimer –
a group effort, they're all resting in peace, it seems,
just as you, newcomer, will also be doing one of these days . . .
But until then, there are things to be done,
as the Schaeffer taxi driver must have told the rearview mirror,
and the rearview mirror repeated, word for word:
art exhibits and panel discussions at Guild Hall,
a Bergmann movie at the Sag Harbor Cinema,
rock-n-roll music in that Amagansett beer parlor,
celebrities with elbows to be rubbed at Bobby Van's,
antique shops to be browsed, a dinner at Gordon's,
poetry readings at the Marine Museum . . .

a busy place the village, once you get away from all those graves:
jumpin' too – you can't rule out a poolside cocktail party
where strangers like yourself are welcomed with open arms
by a host who collects new faces as others collect Ibrim Lassows.
You'll do all that and possibly a lot more more besides
but not until you make your way back to the 1770 House,
stopping off at the bar for a refill before going upstairs
for a shower and a shave, maybe a word to Patrick Henry,
telling him where it was you were just now
and, under no circumstances to accept, if offered death:
all this followed by a nap, perhaps,
one not nearly as long or deep as Hezekiah Brown is having himself
or Mister Fairweather and his goodly wife, Hepzibah . . .
Wake up, newcomer, you've rested long enough, in peace or otherwise:
it's time you made for that front door again
but try to remember not to turn right this time . . .

Antique Chairs, Bridgehampton

Vince Clemente

CLAMMING AT DUSK *for William Heyen*

I

At low tide   prongs of my clamrake
sing under burning stars

I disturb a world underfoot
probing for chowders.

Musselpools like obsidian
blink through sawgrass,

as I probe   prongs of the clamrake
make old stone music

under watching stars.
In the distance   a willet

its wings strung across
the bluff   on fire.

At dusk   the Sound settles into
dumb silence   no sound save the

whisper of my clamrake:
prongs suddenly my own fingers

enter the belly of mudflat,
darkness pulls me in

fingers scale the surface
of seacaves   over the face

of eternal places   ageless
like the silence of the ocean's floor.

II

The flatboat at anchor   rocks
I wake it from sleep   nudge

it into darkness and head
back to Stony Brook Harbor.

With only stars for eyes we glide
oarlocks crack in evening stillness

underbelly of oar becoming my hand:
the black Sound stings   cupped fingers

gather seamoss   grow numb
and clutch the bushel of chowders.

Oars at rest I ride a current
burrow through cattails:

They brush against the boat   whisper
not yet   not yet   not yet.

We rise   as if out of dreams
out of burr reeds   stalks along

the dark channel like girls swaying
fingers pressed to lips.

Sighting shore   the grist mill
its stone wheel dumb:

blue mussels hang like
autumn grapes about to burst.

III

Flatboat beached   I lug
the evening's harvest to shore

chowders fall like moondust   lie
nacreous in black sand,

press one to my lips
lips of the clam sting   briny

sweetness suddenly in my mouth   pull
from my pocket a knife

and shuck the chowder   run my
fingers over its scalloped cheek:

ageless   silent like the walls
of seacaves   old as stone.

Jonathan Cohen

PAUMANOK

The Ocean on the south, and the East river
on the north side which separates this Island
from Manhatans Island as far as Hellgate,
and it is called Paumanok or Long Island,
and runs one-hundred miles of Ocean.

"To say something of the *Indians*," Denton says,
"there's now but few upon the Island and
"those few no ways hurtful to the *English*
"but rather serviceable to them;
"and it is to be admired,
"how strangely they have decreast by the Hand
"of God, since the *English* first came to settle;
"and it hath been generally observed,
"a Divine Hand makes way for the *English*
"removing or cutting off the *Indians*."

They had the gods of the four corners of the earth
— north, south, east and west —
and there was a god over their corn,
another over their beans, pumpkins, and squash;
one god over their homes, another of the fire,
one god over the sea, another of the wind,
one day-god, another was the night-god,
and there were four gods over the four seasons.

And Poggatacut, Sachem of Munhasset, Wayandanch,
Sachem Meuntacut, Momowetow, Sachem of Corchake,
Nowedonah, Sachem of Shinecoke, the said Sachems
having sould unto the worship'll Theophilus Eaton,
Esquire, Governour of the Colony New Haven,
and the worship'll Edward Hopkins, Esquire,
all the Land lyinge from the bounds of the Inhabitants
of Southampton, unto the East side of Napeak,
next unto Meuntacut high Land, with the whole breadth
from Sea to Sea, which the Inhabitants of Southampton
have and do possess, for and in consideration of:

twentie Coats
twentie-four looking glasses
twentie-four hoes
twentie-four hatchets
twentie-four knives
One hundred mugs.

And, in consideration thereof, the forenamed Sachems
doe give upp unto the said Purchasers
all rights and Interest in the said Land,
to them and their heirs forever.

Each made his mark: turtle, snake, buck-horn, skunk.
The sun went down, and a paleface moon hove in sight.

Horses, Bridgehampton

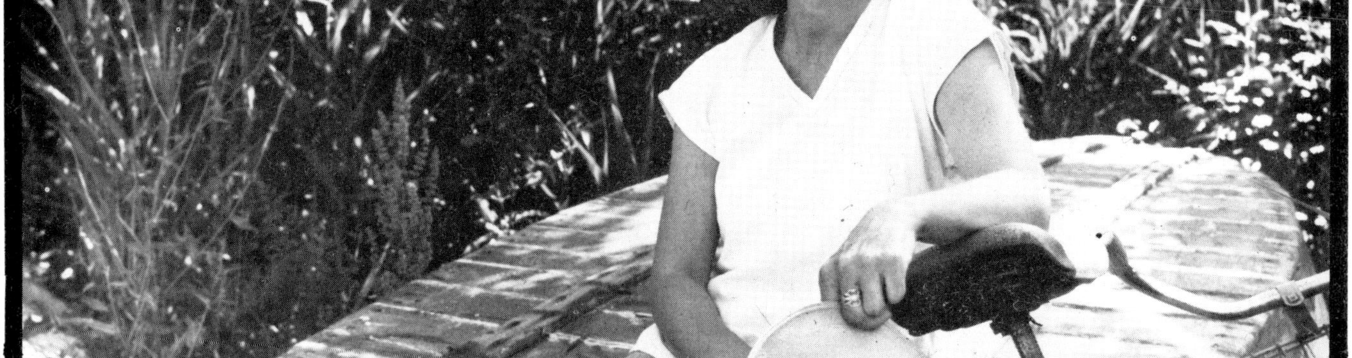

Michele Cusumano

LOVE AFFAIR AND ALTMAN'S

Rites of dress: aisles of silk
furlined gloves, hats with velvet ribbons

She glides down tinsel corridors
tapping the glass counters
What to do?

Until the dream
becomes the wish
becomes the lover
in his wellcut suit.

In his apartment under the bridge
clothes dropped in the dust
crumpled in corners of the bed
Even Altman's can't compete with skin on skin.

Until the afternoons wear thin
and the kisses not so tingly.

Lying draped in bored position
across familiar sheets
she imagines herself in Altman's
a finger caressing a linen sleeve
rub of cashmere
a foot sliding into an Italian shoe.

BLOOD SANDWICHES

Women love blood
It gives us comfort
like bread and new shoes.

Men link it to guns, to car crashes.
We see it by appointment
like the hairdresser.

We pound it into sausage, make it into sandwiches
dipping a crust in the warm juice of the roast.

We make secret pacts with it
stabbing our fingertips
licking off the first drop.

I promise
if I bleed this month
I will buy my mother a toaster
I will get a diaphragm
I will be more careful.

Old Woman Burning Leaves, New Suffolk

Graham Everett

THIRTEEN, FULL OF LIFE

There was a pond we'd fish
off docks of fallen oaks

The fish must have moved out
we used to joke, throwing rocks
at turtles, killing one once
dragging it through the dirt
till its eyes glared us
back to our fishing poles

A Boeing aircraft
broke the sound barrier

heat wove the air
and we smoked dime cigars

THE POTBELLY STOVE

On winter mornings before starting work
the first thing's get a fire going –
paper scraps and kindling flame
the wood chopped, set the flue
and pack a pile for the day

Often tending what matters
the fire goes out
has to be built again, relit

GROOMING FOR DINNER WITH DEATH

There must be some way to trim this beard
and not look so young and scared
sitting at that table, lacking intensity
not having much to say, not very hungry.

Now, hours after midnight
eating everything in sight
in case the call's not to dine

but to be the meat, the guest
stuffed sweet and roasted

bones in the soup stock
eyes in the pudding

Ray Freed

MOOM: 3

In this winter I face my fortieth year
and you gain your eighteenth month.
The raspberry bush is dormant now
where you pulled from its branches
ripe fruit in the summer.

First thing out the back door
you steer your small boots
toward the barren bush,
you do not care winter
denies you fruit

your hands are my hands
our ears hear
winter winds whipping,
the Atlantic surf pounding
on the clear sands.

We go to visit your great grandmother,
whose furrowed face is older
than any flowerings,
more ancient than snow,

and weep, giving her
fresh berries
she can't understand.

SHINNECOCK BAY: 14

I

Again dogwood and forsythia
the bawdy lilacs,
profusion of buds and greens

like the dinosaur Spring
cannot afford the changing earth,
we have taken her territory,

next year the elegant machines
will bring us Spring,
next year Spring will come on schedule.

II

Arcturus, Regulus, Pollux,
counting their measured movement
I doze.

When I rise
six ring-necked mallards
flap off the lapping water

low and parallel to
the moon-mirrored bay.

Birdwatchers, Shinnecock Inlet

David Ignatow

"AS I VIEW THE LEAF. . . "

As I view the leaf, my theme is not the shades of meaning
the mind conveys of it but my desire to make the leaf speak
to me, Chlorophyll, chlorophyll breathlessly, and I would
rejoice with it and in turn say, Blood, and the leaf nod.
Having spoken to each other, the topics would become endless
and, think, as I grow old and the leaf begins to fade and turn
brown, the thought of being buried in the ground would by
then be so familiar, so thoroughly known to me through conver-
sation with the leaf that my walk among the trees after
completing this poem would be like entering my own house.

"I SAW A LEAF FLYING UPWARDS. . ."

I saw a leaf flying upwards from the ground where it had been lying, but there was no wind. Now, how could that be, I asked myself. It was a leaf, shriveled and brittle looking, one of the many hundreds that were falling all about me from off the trees in the woods beside my house and I, puzzled, thinking that perhaps an updraft had caught it and sailed it up into the sky, watched it grow smaller and smaller to the eye, and soon I could not make it out at all. I shrugged and entered my house and closed the door behind me. I could imagine the house beginning to take off too, and I sat down as if to pin it to the earth, and as I sat down there was a short tap on the door. I was expecting company. I walked over and opened the door. A single leaf lay on the doorstep at my feet.

AUTUMN LEAVES

This time I can't grieve
over their deaths in yellow, wine red
and orange. The tree bark is light grey
and a blue jay has just swooped in
to land on a branch, shaking
leaves loose on impact, they
are that weak and insensible
of what's happened. They do
a dance on the air
as they fall.

SLEEPLESS

At this moment two swans in Babylon
shake their feathers of the night
and nestle together among the water thickets,
no happier and no sadder for it either,
but wait as I wait
in this thicket of a room
for the first break in the dark.

Montauk Point Lighthouse

Aaron Kramer

AT NIGHT

All at once the dogs set up a racket
and I know that something's in the street
prowling at the garbage
stirring up the pebbles
fumbling at a lock.

Not a light goes on. Are all the houses
out cold as she is, she beside me
lips unlocked
fingers half unfisted
drawing darkness in like ether through the nostrils
letting a deep dream out?

Suddenly a tread rounds the corner
a tide closes in
a claw pulls down planets
things land, take up position
radios crackle
searchlights violate hedges.

And the street offers nothing in resistance
nothing but this innocuous breathing
and the toothless racket of the dogs.

Norbert Krapf

ARRIVING ON PAUMANOK

Paumanok: *The island with its breast long drawn out.*
W.W., Brooklyn **Standard**

A Midwesterner, an inlander,
a lover of the interior,
arrives on Long Island. "Paumanok!"
he whispers, savoring his Whitman,
local aborigine. "Paumanok," he says,
half aloud. He feels salt water swaying
on every side of him. He looks around
for the rows and rows of ripening
corn he'd sighted down since he was
pushed from the womb. None. Expressways.

"Paumanok," he repeats, looking
at a map. "Manhasset. . . Mineola. . . Massapequa,"
he reads. He picks out names beside
the dots beading the red and green lines
looping the long breast. He turns them
on his tongue like strange herbs.
"Cutchogue. . . Patchogue. . . Ponquogue,"
he intones. "Wantagh and Wickapogue."

He feels a mist drifting in from the shore.
"Quogue and Nissequogue, Nesconsett
and Amagansett," he sings. He hears
the surf splashing nearer. "Commack
and Speonk and Setauket," he chants,
"Ronkonkoma, Ronkonkoma." "Shinnecock,
Peconic." In the middle of a fog
sliding inland off the sea like
the souls of the dead, he says, softly,
"Mattituck, Montauk." He whispers,
"Paumanok, Paumanok." He begins
to hear voices from the interior.

Robert Long

FIRST DAY OF SPRING

My shoes are in their firing-squad position
In the closet. My dog's dead,
But if he were here, he'd be snoring on the floor.
Accidents will happen. If you make them happen,
So much the worse. Yet

Everything goes by so quickly! The first stanza's
Already as ancient as any high school history,
And sudden absences like those leave sudden holes.
When I got cracked in the nose with a baseball bat
Playing grammar school softball,

I saw angels, Lyndon B. Johnson, and doctors
For the next three years, until my nose
Stopped bleeding and started breathing again.
You could say my nose went on strike.
Now it veers toward Portugal

No matter where I'm headed. I'm talking
About my generation, or regeneration.
I saw my best hand-patched jeans
Hit the heap, then reappear, miraculously,
On angels walking down Main Street.

for Lisa Marinaro

SAYING ONE THING

Today, the angels are all writing postcards,
Or talking on the telephone.
Meanwhile, in Nowheresville,
A rabbit is running into a bush. This, I tell my friend,
Means good luck. The next day,
The sun is out, the fix is in,

And we're ready to throw in the towel.
Anytime now, our number might come up,
And the telephone will finally stop ringing:
Don't call before three,
Knock four times,
Show me the way to go home,

Back and forth and back again,
Like some idiot boomerang.
"Kerpow" and "schlock" are our favorite words,
Lately, and are about what things are amounting to.
Still, the stories of airplane disasters
And overnight flings in faroff cities have a kind of allure,

Like metallic paint, or something expensive
You want but can't have.
O toothpaste commercials, common house fly,
Fall is in the air again. On this spaceship
The code word is "blonde," or "good dog."
Night begins to fall, the atmosphere is electric.

for Daisy Jacobs

Antique Car, Cutchogue

Dan Murray

AUGUST

Sitting on the porch I shuffle the cards,
days flicker by like a picket fence.
Over gin and dispersed dandelion,
and leaves fizzing chartreuse,
innocence goes to seed.

Sunset inflames the evening haze.
Moths twitch around the lightbulb,
pleading another dream,

and it must be rest
the locusts crave all night.

OCTOBER

Bless the flourish of auburn hills,
& the leap of white-tail deer.

Bless the plainsong of the wind
veering toward abandon.

Bless the boast of oak & birch,
& the wishbones of their branches.

A TOAST TO THE JUDGE

I sink into a topless bar.
Amaretto & the body riffs
drift me into the dream:

I want a woman
who hears my poems,
then speaks her own intimacy,
naked recognition.

The dancer winks about New Year's
Eve in Coney Island bumper cars,
making it on a rug of braided mink.
Pleasure steers her strange canoe,
& Dylan sings *Just Like A Woman.*

She wants a dollar for the jukebox.
I sit in the dust of the pony express.

Ron Overton

PRIVATE EYE

He is an owl.

A gorgeous knock will come
& summon him from his perch above
the stale reek of coffee cups
& old butts & out
into the bitter public street,
the urban dark he loves for this:
just the stains of crime stand out.
With the lamp of his contempt
he scours the night,
everything is relevant.
Clues mew like mice.
So he finds this scree of a life:
a torn snapshot, some broken glass, a tooth.

The case is closed.

*　　　*　　　*

That he is lord
of the confused & small he knows.
He thinks nine ways at once
for the widow with the one-track mind.
He mends the puzzle pieces
of what the rich have blindly smashed.
He is the ruddy brain that mocks
the muscle of the law.
He is the master
of all permutations of deceit.
His eye can get inside.

*　　　*　　　*

Disguised,
risk thrilled,
he slips down among the catacombs of crime.
Who can survive this murky hell?
Two days & he's back,
twirling his ruby stickpin:
wise, untouched,
casual in revelation.

He would take fear in his throat
like smoke deliberately inhaled too deep,
then toss it out
as laughter.

He would keep things lean.
The cheaper the crook, the gaudier the patter.

He would be
just a little fancier than death.

Camper, Hampton Bays

Simon Perchik

TODAY I WILL PREPARE THE GROUND

Today I will prepare the ground
stomp every flower in this park
– those that re-group
cut their stems. Only these
will I bring.

Nothing heavier.
You won't need their roots
or dirt – I will bury
public flowers. Your dreams
– forget it! nothing goes

but you.
I will train your feet
to knock, to loosen the hard reds
mined all Spring
– I will make a scene

but you? won't lift a hand
will be arranged, styled
for that varnished, endless vase
– these flowers will be taught.
Everybody will be punished.

What I bring
will never rise again :my eyes
unable to lift you
under these mangled blooms.

THE FRONT GATE

The front gate
unlocked, I steal
its fence. The paint too
ajar. Nothing's closed, pickets
missing :my teeth
raid the porch, a house
worn thin from theft.

I must find someplace.
My feet are empty.

Home Port, Port Jefferson

Allen Planz

METRO *for Ray Freed*

There is love
& maybe I call it great
because nothing
else
keeps me going day
into night. Heading west
on the Long Island plains
New York's skyline
seems unchanging
all thru my life
the thrill I got
as a kid
still with me:
it was promised I'd love it.

The city invents
speech. I take the BMT uptown,
the shuffle east
or is it north? & emerge
where even the graffiti
has evolved beyond me,
only a number & a glyph.
But I talk to changemakers
or pedestrians, muggers or
mothers. Though I've been lost
for days, they always tell
me what I need to know.

The city invents
me decade
into decade. My speech
is late
twentieth century American
New York, drunk or dishonest
metropolitan
knowing myself
only by what I say with other New Yorkers
meaning survival
& proud in the terror & splendor of it.

City of my birth
& death of those I knew,
parents & loved ones, friends & neighbors,
I can again
& again
walk the archway of the city's tilt
knowing what was said survives as they meant it.
It was promised them too.

Beach Chairs, Bridgehampton

Carol Sherman

SAG HARBOR

Honeysuckle climbs the old wood fence
circles the house
The chestnut tree stubborn and tall,
shades the yard
Seagulls fly overhead
gliding in the bay breeze
The house, old and scarred,
Needs a chance to start again
Paint...new shutters
a carpenter with a loving heart.

What will become of us,
ghosts in the corners
Our tears and laughter
like lemon oil in the woodwork
With never a witness
left to tell
Of the band concerts in the harbor
Of the pretty girl next door
in her summer dress
Our voices whisper
We will never die
...never die.

But we'll be gone.
No matter we loved at Pierson High
Or that I fought in Normandy
and wrote you love letters everyday.
The pink satin pillow
I sent your mother from Fort Bragg
Sits in its box in the corner
waiting to be found by strangers.
No matter we loved or cared –
The blue and white band uniform
a mute witness to
The music of our love
our lives.

Louis Simpson

THE BEADED PEAR

Kennst du das Land, wo die Zitronen blüh'n?
Goethe, "Mignon"

1 Shopping

Dad in Bermuda shorts, Mom her hair in curlers,
Jimmy, sixteen, and Darlene who is twelve,
are walking through the Smith Haven Mall.

Jimmy needs a new pair of shoes.
In the Mall by actual count
there are twenty-two stores selling shoes:
Wise Shoes, Regal Shoes,
National Shoes, Naturalizer Shoes,
Stride Rite, Selby, Hanover . . .

Dad has to buy a new lock for the garage,
Mom and Darlene want to look at clothes.
They agree to meet again in an hour
at the fountain.

The Mall is laid out like a cathedral
with two arcades that cross –
Macy's at one end of the main arcade,
Abraham and Straus at the other.

At the junction of transept and nave
there is a circular, sunken area
with stairs where people sit,
mostly teenagers, smoking
and making dates to meet later.
This is what is meant by "at the fountain."

2 *"Why don't you get transferred, Dad?"*

One of Jimmy's friends comes by in his car,
and Jimmy goes out. "Be careful,"
Mom says. He has to learn to drive,
but it makes her nervous thinking about it.

Darlene goes over to see Marion
whose father is being transferred
to a new branch of the company
in Houston. "Why don't you get transferred, Dad?"

"I'd like to," he replies.
"I'd also like a million dollars."

This is a constant topic in the family:
where else would you like to live.
Darlene likes California –

"It has beautiful scenery
and you get to meet all the stars."
Mom prefers Arizona, because of a picture
she saw once, in **Good Housekeeping.**
Jimmy doesn't care,
and Dad likes it here. "You can find anything
you want right where you are."
He reminds them of **The Wizard of Oz**,
about happiness, how it is found
right in your own backyard.

Dad's right, Mom always says.
The Wizard of Oz is a tradition
in the family. They see it every year.

3 The Beaded Pear

The children are home at six,
and they sit down to eat. Mom insists
on their eating together at least once
every week. It keeps the family together.

After helping with the dishes
the children go out again,
and Mom and Dad settle down to watch
"Hollywood Star Time," with Bobby Darin,
Buddy Rich, Laura Nyro,
Judy Collins, and Stevie Wonder.

When this is over he looks in **TV Guide**,
trying to decide
whether to watch "Salty O'Rourke (1945).
A gambler who is readying his horse
for an important race
falls in love with a pretty teacher,"
or, "Delightful family fare,
excellent melodrama of the Mafia."

She has seen enough television
for one night. She gets out the beaded pear
she bought today at the Mall.

A "Special $1.88 do-it-yourself Beaded Pear.
No glueing or sewing required.
Beautiful beaded fruit is easily assembled
using enclosed pins, beads, and decorative material."

She says, "It's not going to be so easy."

"No," he says, "it never is."

Ruth Swensen

LIVING INSIDE MY BODY

I try to get out
with tricks of imagination.
Great geese sleeping on mud flats
flight filled.
Specters of winter trees.
I have learned to turn myself inside
but not out.

With you I climb trees taller than Sunday afternoon.
Deer watch us from thickets, underbrush.
Salmon chronicle our swim towards some foamy death.

But until that time
when split sky drops ocean deep
and mourning fish hurl themselves at the sun,
there is, in the space between us,
not just the touch of skin,
but a singing, an ancient sound,
heard down deep hearted rivers.

Jim Tyack

THE INVISIBLE ROSE

Wait I say it.
Something has to be settled here.
She says: *We have an understanding.*
Share a responsibility.
I say: *Marriage is sacred.*
Like a cow.

the landscape we stand in
gets busy
loses its pastoral simplicity
clouds materialize in the distance
rivers evaporate before our eyes.

Rothko said:
start with nothing
& let it grow

& the paint grows thick on my feet
the omelets burn & curl like frisbees
the refrigerator humming
a white nostalgic emblem
the mirror in the hall
filled with invisible roses
the shadowy gracelessness of television
& the telephone

I take everything
I ever had to offer her
out to lunch
& get it drunk

the waitress
the busboy
the hatcheck girl
laughing

my 7th martini iced to death rattling
each nerve cauterized & jumpy as a tick in scrub oak
the distant rivers gone

SHADOW

At home
in the darkroom
the negative shimmers

the print is nothing
but a shadow

perhaps a heavy hand
touching a tendril
inside the head

It could have been anything
a plane's wing
fire of a dancing saint

the two of us
walking across a lawn
at a party on Long Island

me yawning
you lighting a cigarette

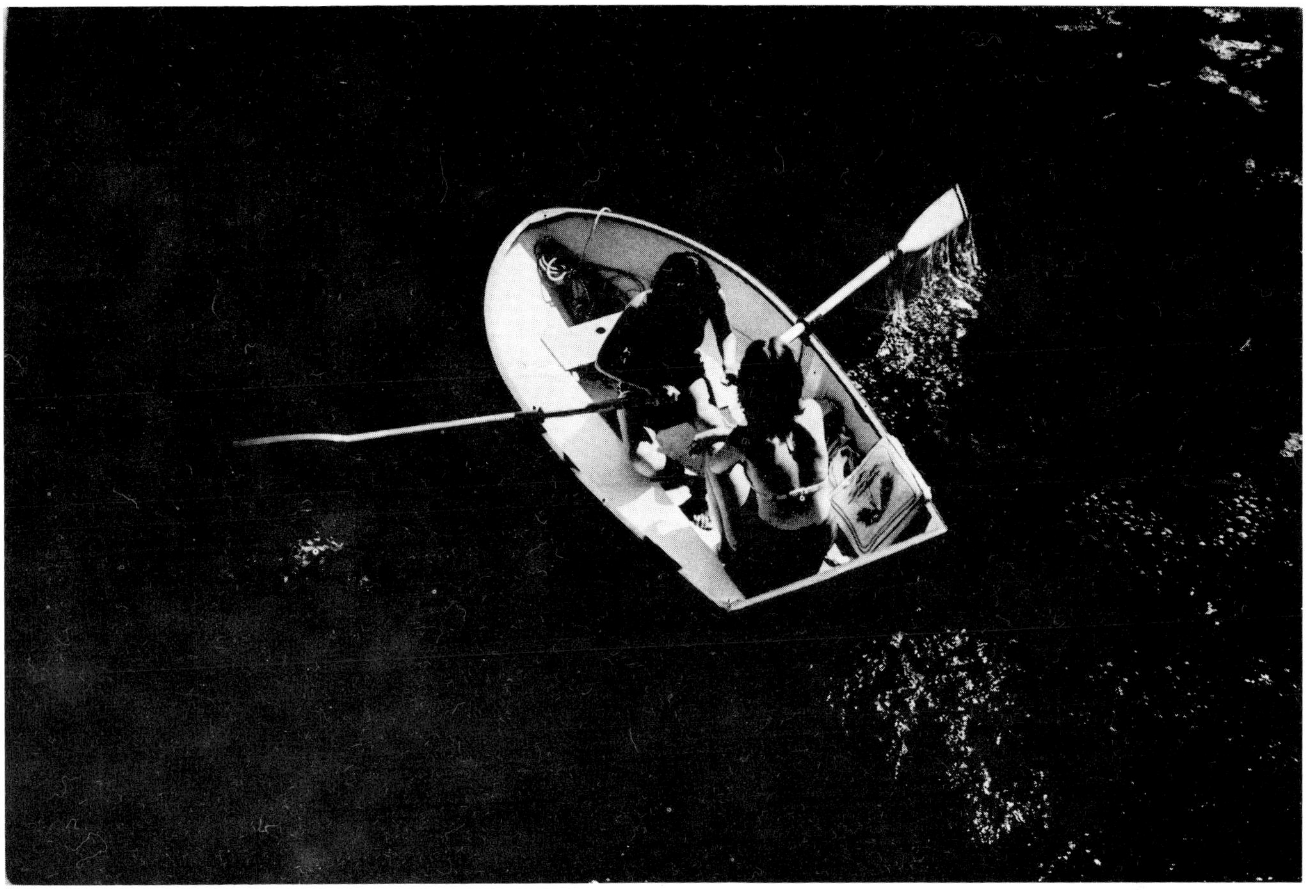

Girls in Rowboat, Mattituck

Jeanne Voege

THE WHALES IN NEW YORK HARBOR

Grandpa heard them
sighing long soft breezes
in Delaware, the Chesapeake
and San Francisco Bay
in all the inlets of the world
from great deep journeys
they rested, serene and snoring

It was the Right Whale
Grandpa said, all but gone
within one hundred years
Far away it pulsates now
the lonely call
Another to touch, to answer
Where are the others, it cries

I feel it pounding
seabottom wave to shore
reaching
depths of memory
core to the edge and back

The song engulfs me flowing
through and around me soothing
endless sounds from the womb
and my voice
too small to answer

R.B. Weber

SUMMER ALONG THE PECONIC

after storms   the raindust smell
and the earth spinning   in the clean
celled   sunsheen   with water
dripping   in and out   and down
among the leaves   styled green.
And the rough   black   bark   kept
moist and gleaming ebony awhile.
As summer, on the death of afternoon,
upon the verge of night   dooms
a rabble throng of thunderheads;
their long   jagged   yellow   spears
distanced down,shafts aground.
Spinning as a sunflecke'd haze
that watered dust   holds countless
days   countenances of our
dreams,   those pale,stiff,smiling
faces   once flicked by lovestung
lips   once brushed by groping
fingertips. And now   only now
those dim scenes hover   late late
into the still   still suburban purple
bandaging   the garden chairs.

BEHIND THESE LIDS

as I lie back
my eyes float
below the top of my face:
two deep closed wells,
boarded over now.
I hear from the wind
at the edge of the windows,
muttering through the mesh:
from the south it keeps
saying *from the south.*

A long time ago
I saw what it said:
my eyes opened ponds
birds flew around –
snow geese and loons,
sparrows and blue birds,
crows and cardinals –
But now who sees
what the wind says?
My eyes shutter shut.

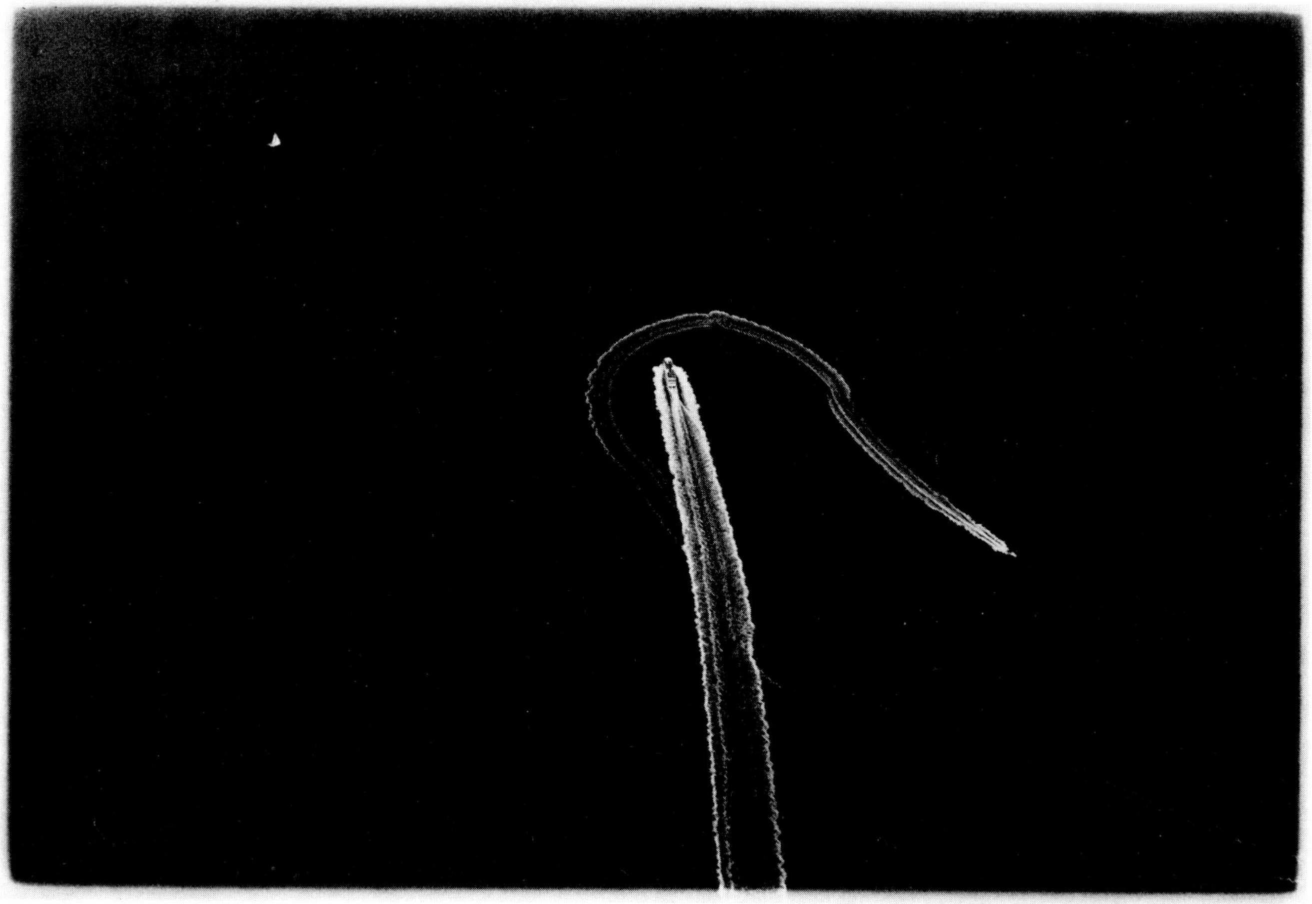

Fire Island Ferry, Bayshore

Claire Nicolas White

DRIVING NORTH ON NICOLL'S ROAD

All this one can manage:
the reddish weeds on the road divider,
the dry rust of scrub oak against
the intense mauve of the sky.

The thread of a cobweb glistens
across the windshield, parallel
to the contrail of a jet plane.
The yellow school bus ahead

echoes the yellow line painted
on the road. Behind it lies
the school with its hot bodies,
an occasional tooth missing.

But ahead menaces the black
health-sciences building, a huge
blind processing plant, sucking up
footloose creatures for miles around.

LIVES

Lives have no shape till they're ended.
Imagine the fish without its tail,
That open mouth, drinking in the whole sea,

the eyes looking away from each other,
the gills pumping out what came in,
all those scales, do they form a pattern?

But the tail propels it onward,
holds it together, steers its course.
The fish becomes an arrow.

MICHAEL BRAUDE

A graduate of The University of Denver and author of the play *Gettysburg,* which was produced on National Educational Television. His poetry and short stories have appeared in *Commentary, Harper's Magazine, Shenandoah,* and other magazines and periodicals. Mr. Braude now lives in East Hampton and is at work on the second volume of his autobiography, to be published by Horizon Press.

VINCE CLEMENTE

An Associate Professor of English at Suffolk Community College and founding editor of *West Hills Review: A Walt Whitman Journal,* he is the author of *Songs From Puccini* and *Snow Owl Above Stony Brook Harbor.* His poems and essays have appeared in *Kansas Quarterly, The New York Times,* and *Red Cedar Review,* among others. He lives in Setauket with his wife Annie and their daughters, Mary Ann and Gina.

JONATHAN COHEN

Author of *Poems From The Island,* Jonathan Cohen lives in Port Jefferson. His poetry has appeared in many magazines as well as in *The New York Times.* He also translates Spanish American poets, and New Directions has published two books which include his translations of Enrique Lihn (1978) and Ernesto Cardenal (1980). He teaches in the English Department of Stony Brook University.

MICHELE CUSUMANO

Came to the East End six years ago from a brownstone in Brooklyn. Her first job was tying cauliflower for a local farmer. Now working as a welfare examiner for Suffolk County, in addition to being father, mother, housekeeper and provider for three factious teenagers. A forthcoming book, *Just As The Boy Dreams of White Thighs Under Flowered Skirts,* is being published by Street Press.

GRAHAM EVERETT

Born and bred on the East End, his work has appeared in numerous magazines and periodicals. *Strange Coast* was published by Tamarack Editions in 1979, and he is currently at work on a manuscript entitled *Rage, Lust & Hunger*, as well as being active in the Poets-in-the-Schools program.

RAY FREED

A poet and editor, he lives in Westhampton Beach with his wife Joann and son Phil. His poems have appeared in *Descant, The Georgia Review, Prism International, unmuzzled ox,* and other magazines and periodicals. *MOOM,* a chapbook, was published by Street Press in 1979.

DAVID IGNATOW

Poet-In-Residence at York College, City University of New York. His latest volume of poems, *Tread The Dark,* appeared from Atlantic, Little-Brown, in 1978, and most recently he has published *Open Between Us,* a collection of interviews and essays, from The University of Michigan Press.

AARON KRAMER

A Professor of English at Dowling College, Mr. Kramer has published extensively, most recently *Carousel Parkway,* and is also known as a translator, into English, of Yiddish and German poets. He lives in Oakdale.

NORBERT KRAPF

An Associate Professor of English at C.W. Post College of Long Island University, he is the author of two poetry chapbooks, *The Playfair Book Of Hours* and *Arriving On Paumanok.* He is expanding his ancestral miscellany, *Finding The Grain*, during 1980-81 while serving as Senior Fulbright Lecturer in American Literature at the University of Freiburg, Germany. In 1981 Ally Press will publish his narrative cycle *Lines Drawn From Dürer.*

ROBERT LONG

He lives in East Hampton, is 25, and has had work appear in *The New Yorker, Partisan Review, Poetry,* and other magazines. *What It Is,* a chapbook of poems with drawings by Eileen O'Kane, is about to be released by Street Press.

DAN MURRAY

Short Circuits, a book of poems, was published by Street Press in 1976, and *The Calendar Poems* were privately printed in 1977. His work has recently appeared in *Gravida, Street Magazine,* and *West Hills Review.* He is a Professor of English at Suffolk Community College and has lived on the East End for the past fifteen years.

RON OVERTON

Lives in Lake Grove with his wife, son, and an enormous goldfish. He was the recipient of an NEA Fellowship in 1976-77. He is an avid reader of mystery novels, such as Hammet's *The Maltese Falcon,* from which the quote in "Private Eye" is taken. His most recent book is *Dead Reckoning*, Street Press, 1979.

SIMON PERCHIK

This poet's work has appeared in *Massachusetts Quarterly, The Nation, Poetry, Poetry Northwest, Texas Quarterly*, and elsewhere. Born in 1923, he has published six books of poetry, is married, lives in East Hampton, and is a practicing attorney.

ALLEN PLANZ

Past poetry editor of *The Nation,* his work has been published in a wide variety of books and periodicals. He is a fisherman who lives in East Hampton and a regional coordinator of the Poets-in-the-Schools Program. His books include *A Night For Rioting, Wildcraft,* and *Chunderhara.*

CAROL SHERMAN

A fashion designer with her own shop in Southampton, her poems have appeared in several magazines, as well as the anthology *East of Shinnecock.* She lives in Shinnecock Hills with her husband and three cats.

LOUIS SIMPSON

A resident of Port Jefferson, his new book of poems, *Caviare At The Funeral,* has just been published by Franklin Watts. In 1980-81 he will be away from Long Island, in Hawaii until Christmas and then in Pittsburgh.

RUTH SWENSEN

Has published poems and stories in various literary magazines, including *Street* and *The Hamptons.* She lives in East Hampton with a husband, sons, and assorted animals.

JIM TYACK

Born and raised on Long Island, his work has appeared in *Street Magazine, Down Here, The Village Voice, Prairie Schooner, Newsday, Bird Effort,* and elsewhere. A book of poems, *The Rented Tuxedo,* was published by Street Press in 1976.

JEANNE VOEGE

A resident of Westhampton, she has published more than fifty poems in various literary and local magazines and periodicals in the last six years, and performed her poetry in over twenty public readings. She is also the founder and past director of the Association of Local Poets, ALPS.

R. B. WEBER

His work has appeared in *Long Pond Review, Chelsea, Poetry Now, The Nation, Bird Effort, Kansas Quarterly,* and elsewhere. His latest book, *Poems From The Xenia Hotel,* was published by Street Press in 1979. He is a Professor of English at Southampton College of Long Island University.

CLAIRE NICOLAS WHITE

Her poems have appeared in *The New Yorker, Paris Review, Harper's Magazine, Atlantic Monthly, Saturday Review of Literature, Sumac,* and others. Doubleday will publish *Biography and Other Poems* in the spring of 1981. She has lived in St. James since 1947.

RON RIBEIRO

Lives in Westhampton Beach, where he is employed as a house painter. He is a freelance photographer who has worked for a weekly East End newspaper since September, 1977.